Oh My Goddess

Oh My Goddess

poems

by

April Bulmer

Serengeti Press

Published by: Serengeti Press
              193 Church St., P.O. Box 146
              Oakville, Ontario L6J 4Z5

Canadian Cataloguing in Publication Data
ISBN 0-9732068-4-5

      1. Title
PS8553.U49O38 2004   C811'.54   C2004-905162-8

Bulmer, April: 1963 -
      Oh My Goddess: poems

Cover Art: © Melanie Davis
            of Valkyria Fine Art and Jewellery

Cover Design by Stella Mazur Preda (Serengeti Press)

Printed and bound in Canada by E-Impressions

Acknowledgements

Thank you to Stella Mazur Preda at Serengeti Press; the editors who have published some of the poems in this chapbook; my mother; the spirit of my father; Kirk, Stephanie, Karen; the Cambridge Writers Collective; John B. Lee; Marty Gervais of Black Moss Press; Trinity College; Dr.Norman King of the University of Windsor; Trinity Church, Cambridge and Bear.

Contents

When our Goddess is voluptuous, erotic,
so will be our dances,
the rhythms of our drums and chants,
our bodies.

Starhawk: *Truth or Dare*

Freya, Norse Goddess of Love

Sometimes we rested beneath the winter sun; he offered me praise and hymns. I pressed myself against the old ache of his body, kissed the blood and sea salt from his lips. I emptied myself into his dreams and his helmet shifted as he slept.

But one day he sailed and he would not worship, nor call upon me in the cold hull of his ship. He rocked against the hard bones of his vessel, but would not love me in the damp night air.

I remembered the coarse weave of his garments, his thick braids of hair... his ritual prayers and sacrifice under a full-horned moon.

One day I laid down and the sun made a shadow of me: against that tablet of earth I am a scar: a rune.

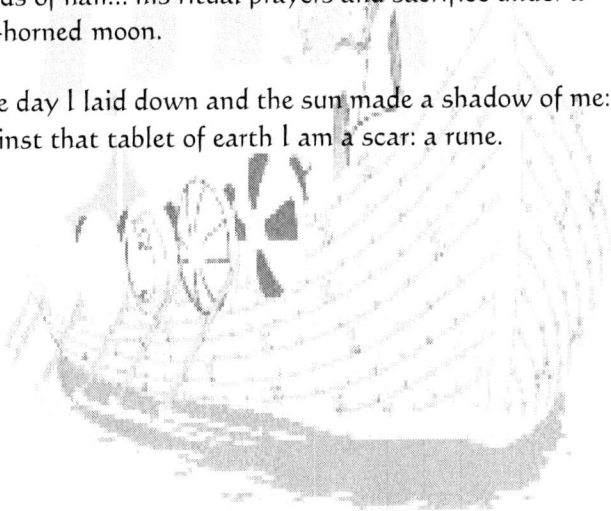

The Norns - Norse Goddess of Fate

When the soil is dry and limbs broken my sisters and I
bear water to the tree.* We circle the trunk round and
round, the girls and I. Then Urd glances behind her and
Skuld, veiled, clutches a little bound book. While I rest
upon the shadows and the great ash, whispering the fate
of light and leaves.

*The great tree, Yggdrasil, gave the universe its stability. The
Norns packed and cared for the earth surrounding its three
mighty roots, while the evil serpent Nidhogg continually
gnawed on one of them, hoping one day to bite through and
thereby cause the universe to fall into chaos.

The Witch at Endor

King Saul outlawed all sorcery and divination - said no.
But later prayed for a prophet, a dream.

He came to me and so we knelt at a small shrine of fire.
I woke King Samuel's sleeping spirit and he stumbled
into my tent, rubbing the vision from his eyes.

I killed a fatted calf, kneaded and baked unleavened
bread. I fed Saul knowing he would pound his life like
dough.

Elizabeth, Mother of John the Baptist

Gabriel's perfect mouth a trumpet, a sudden tune: fear
not, Zechariah, your wife shall bear a son and he will
make ready a people prepared for the Messiah. My
husband's eyes stuttered remembering my old breasts,
their abandoned croon. He would not believe, shouted no.
The angel's anger a taut bow: Zechariah stumbled mute
from the temple. His tongue quivered, his hands too, still
dusty with incense. When he touched me he could not call
my name, could not touch and say Elizabeth, my wife,
yes. My bones were slim canes, my hair thin as breath,
and my woman's blood only a memory, a dark shadow in
the shallow valley of my womb. But I dreamed a pool of
water and the boy leapt in me – a weight we carried like
jugs from the river. When the waters shifted, I laboured
and brought forth. Days later at the briss, our son's
name – John – fell like a drop of rain from Zechariah's
dry tongue.

Mary, Mother of Jesus the Christ

And he trembles in me like a new dove in a cage of frail
bone; trembles as the Holy Spirit trembled the morning
we nested. I am betrothed now and some nights Joseph
touches me, my breasts white and new as desert blooms.
We do not speak of the fullness of God, the burden of
grace, the weight of love. But in dreams Joseph saws the
days into planks, long slivered planks stained with water
and blood.

Woman With the Flow of Blood

I offered turtledoves and pigeons; healers and midwives a heavy sack of coins. Still the old snake shed her red skins. Her woman cloth. At night, she dragged her long belly through my tent and into the dry thighs of the desert. In dreams Jesus beat across the sand as a raven, taking the snake limp in his beak; snagged his soft wings in a tree. But in the morning my body was a weak basket where the blood coiled. And the men did not play their pipes for me.

Twelve years I bled. My spirit so weak, but still the dreams flew.

The day Jesus crossed over the sea, I went to him in the crowd and I did reach out and touch a tassel that hung from his garment. The snake opened her wide jaw and pulled her thick tail into herself: my womb was firm and healthy as an apple.

And he praised the tight knot of my faith: the dreams that did not crawl away from my heart, nor slough my body.

Pilate's Wife

Too late when I groaned and the dream slipped from me, a
black cord loose round its wet throat. A noose Pontius cut
like a midwife, his hands thin as knives, and delivered to
the festival. My breasts were jars of milk curdled in the
hot sun as the priests, the elders abandoned my dream.
Rattled their death charms.

They led Jesus away, his hips slender but his belly swollen
like a woman's, bearing a weight and a skein of rope
knotted to God. Slack to grasp, though our hands are
blades still wet with blood.

Ursula*

The visions were frequent
and did frighten you.

The documents do not mention
a Mama or Papa.
Only a husband some say was crazed.
(Lienhold was his name.)
And a daughter, Elsa.

I would stand you by the Rhine
and offer you the chance to say
whether baptism was indeed your way.
So many died for this "crime,"
this belief.

I want to know
did they drown you too?
Did the river waters bless you
or gather in grief?

* Ursula Jost was an Anabaptist woman who lived in the early
sixteenth century in Strasbourg, Germany. Thousands of
Anabaptists were tortured and put to death for their rejection
of infant baptism and for their belief that adults should be
baptized after a confession of faith. It is not known how or
when Ursula died or even if she was arrested.

We do know that Ursula became well known in Strasbourg and
throughout Holland for her prophetic visions. She was a
member of a small, well-recognized group called the Strasbourg
Prophets. The group met to discuss visions and religious
concerns. Ursula's visions were colourful and apocalyptic in
nature. They were organized and published in 1530. Copies of
this booklet still exist in Munich and Zurich.

Julian *

You lived in a cell
in the village of Connisford
in Norwich, England.
From a window you could see
the church altar
and watch the confessions of sins.
Unmarried, you were an anchor, a soul friend.
You offered solace and comfort
to parishioners and pilgrims.

At age 30, you received visions:
Jesus as Mother, but still Christ.

Was he gripped in love as in childbirth?
Bore us blood, water and newness of life?

* St. Julian of Norwich was an anchoress who lived in solitude at
the Church of St. Julian in Norwich, England in the late
fourteenth century (1342-1416). During a severe illness, she
received 16 "shewings" or revelations of God's love. She wrote
two versions of these visions. The first was a short text. The
second, longer version, was written some years later after she had
time to pray and reflect about the teachings God had given her.

Julian of Norwich wrote in an unpretentious manner and her
theology was precise without being pedantic. She had a gift for
expressing profound thoughts in simple language. Her book
Showings revealed that she experienced God as Mother. This
expression of the feminine aspect of God represented a
significant contribution to the Christian tradition.

Cinderella

I wore low pumps, but my feet throbbed.

I worked afternoons at a haberdashery. Wrapped bars of
soap in tissue and tied them with dark ribbon. Dabbed
colognes and waters on the thick wrists of gentlemen.

I never touched him as I touched my customers. Never
rubbed his rough hands with lotions and creams. Never
smoothed his wild curls with hair oils.

I did not desire his arms, his steady pulse, only the
strange delight of that dark hollow.

I told him I wanted hot water and my old porcelain tub.
That I was a kind of turtle who required the protection of
its white shell, its four sturdy claws.

He watched me bathe by candlelight. Even reached out
and took the cake of oatmeal and glycerine from my hand,
washed my soft underbelly.

Then I wet the wick; soaked in steam and darkness. I felt
the long lay of his tongue. The suck of his teeth. My toes
were round and swollen as grapes, he desired their sweet
wine.

He'd walked for years, his suede boots kicking the dust.

One evening: the gentle push of my ankle, the pull of his
lips.

His mouth; a fine slipper, a comfortable fit.

Our Ladies

But I am a beauty like you, Mama, they say, and hold my slight hands your way. And Aunt is also steeped deep in me.

In fact, there are three Mothers to love and with whom I may speak, for there is Our Lady too.

Tonight I honour her thighs with daisies and cries. It is dusk, and birds have come to rest in her shadows and in her bedroom of light.

Sins

In the dim, you lift
Mary in your weak and
boyish arms. For the
Mother of God
is light.

You do not visit me again.
You are on your knees
making love to the church.

You have never entered
a woman, you say.
You think that place
is like a wound.
I think you are right.

Black Madonna

Blowing smoke up the virgin:
the way she drags the shadow.

The wind caresses
her stony thighs now.
I laud her
with curtsies
and sighs.

She wants
the smell of a man
on my palms and sleeves.

Curses the Sisters
who drink their milk
to her purity and grief.

Woman

When the fullness of time
had come
God did not send
a daughter or son
or milk sticky and sour
on my bosom.
"Blessed are the barren,"
He said instead.

Creed

A cardinal at the bird feeder,
early June.
Balanced on the ledge.
Pecking at the hard seeds.

He opens his red wings
and blooms.

Seeds

Moon flower opens at night
the way I do.
Are women born
from the mucky root
of all blossoms and trees?
Water and light too?

Credits

Some of these poems have appeared in
Contemporary Verse 2, Arc,
Voices and Visions Vol. 6
(Winning Poems and Others from the Waterloo-
Wellington CAA Poetry Contest 2002),
Kaleidoscope, and *Leaving Footprints.*

Biography

April Bulmer has published three books of poetry: *A Salve For Every Sore* (Cormorant Books), *The Weight of Wings* (Trout Lily Press), and *HIM* (Black Moss Press).

She has four university degrees, including Masters Degrees in Creative Writing, Religious Studies and Theology. She has been published in many journals including the *Malahat Review, Arc, Prism, Contemporary Verse 2* and *Vox Feminarum*.

Her work has also been included in a number of Black Moss Press anthologies, most recently a woman's book entitled Leaving Footprints.

In 1998, she was nominated for the Pat Lowther Award for the best book of poetry by a Canadian woman. April lives in Cambridge, Ontario.